Materials

Rock

Cassie Mayer

Heinemann
LIBRARY

www.heinemann.co.uk/library
Visit our website to find out more information about Heinemann Library books.

To order:
☎ Phone 44 (0) 1865 888066
🖹 Send a fax to 44 (0) 1865 314091
🖳 Visit the Heinemann Bookshop at www.heinemann.co.uk/library to browse our catalogue and order online.

First published in Great Britain by Heinemann Library, Halley Court, Jordan Hill, Oxford OX2 8EJ, part of Pearson Education. Heinemann is a registered trademark of Pearson Education Ltd.

Editorial: Diyan Leake
Design: Joanna Hinton-Malivoire
Picture research: Tracy Cummins and Heather Mauldin
Production: Duncan Gilbert

Originated by Chroma Graphics (Overseas) Pte Ltd
Printed and bound in China by South China Printing Co. Ltd

ISBN 978 0 431 19259 8
12 11 10 09 08
10 9 8 7 6 5 4 3 2 1

British Library Cataloguing in Publication Data
Mayer, Cassie
  Rock. - (Materials)
  1. Rocks - Juvenile literature
  I. Title
  620.1'32

Acknowledgments
The author and publisher are grateful to the following for permission to reproduce copyright material: © Corbis p. **15** (Remi Benali/Corbis); © Getty Images p. **7** (Richard Drury); © Heinemann Raintree pp. **4**, **6**, **9**, **11**, **17**, **18**, **19**, **20**, **21**, **22** (David Rigg); © Istockphoto p. **10** (Justin Horrocks); © Peter Arnold p. **12** (Mark Edwards); © Shutterstock pp. **5** (Geir Olav Lyngfjell), **8** (Perov Stanislav), **13** (Cecilia Lim H M), **14** (Marco Rametta), **16** (Feverpitched), **23** (Marco Rametta).

Cover image used with permission of © Getty Images (D. Steele/Photo Access). Back cover image used with permission of © Heinemann Raintree (David Rigg).

Every effort has been made to contact copyright holders of any material reproduced in this book. Any omissions will be rectified in subsequent printings if notice is given to the publisher.

Contents

What is rock?

Rock is a material.

It is found in the world around us.

Rocks come in many colours.

Rocks come in many sizes.

Rocks come in many shapes.

Some rock is hard.

Granite is a hard rock.

Some rock is soft.

Chalk is a soft rock.

Rocks can be big.

Rocks can be small.

Where are rocks found?

Rocks are found above the ground.

Rocks are found below the ground.

You can see rocks on a beach.

You can see rocks under water.

You can see rocks in fields.

This house is in between two rocks.

Can rocks change?

The wind can change the shape of rocks.

The sea can change the shape
of rocks.

How do people use rocks?

Rocks are used to make buildings.

Rocks are used to make jewellery.

Types of rock

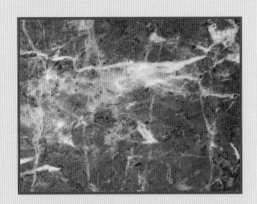 ◀marble

 ▲diamond

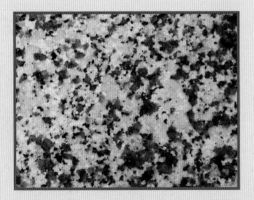 ◀granite

Picture glossary

 **beach** area near water. Beaches are covered with sand and rocks.

 **field** open area of land

 **sea** the salt water that covers most of the Earth. Over a long time, the sea can wear rock away.

Content vocabulary for teachers

material something that can be used to make things

Index

Notes for parents and teachers

Before reading   Put items made of materials such as wood, plastic, metal, rock, and rubber in a closed bag. Challenge the children to feel in the bag and, without looking, identify the object made of rock. What did it feel like? Was it cold to touch? Is it heavy? Talk about rocks. Have the children ever picked up pebbles on a beach? Have they every climbed over a big rock?

After reading

• Give each child a pebble and some poster paints. Tell them to paint a face on the pebble. Encourage them to use the natural curve of the pebble for features such as the nose or an ear.

• Invite children to bring in different examples of small rocks. Help the children to sort them; for example, by colour or feel.